CAMERA, WOMAN
A play in two parts

R.M. Vaughan

COACH HOUSE BOOKS

Published with the assistance of the Canada Council for the Arts
and the Ontario Arts Council

Conseil des Arts du Canada
The Canada Council

ONTARIO ARTS
COUNCIL
CONSEIL DES ARTS
DE L'ONTARIO

CANADIAN CATALOGUING IN PUBLICATION DATA

Vaughan, R.M. (Richard Murray), 1965-
  Camera, woman

ISBN 1-55245-055-4

1. Arzner, Dorothy, 1900-1979 – Drama. I. Title.

PS8593.A94C35 2000   C812'.54   C00-932540-9
PR199.3.V389C35 2000

for Franco Boni

Characters

DOROTHY ARZNER – early 40s, black hair, costumed in men's clothing, educated American accent.

MERLE OBERON – early 20s, English actress, delicate features.

HARRY COHN – late 50s, Jewish, costumed in expensive suits.

LOUELLA PARSONS – early 50s, Midwestern accent, overdressed in florid costumes.

ROSE LINDSTROM – mid 30s, blonde, costumed in loud dresses.

PAM COOK – late 20s, costumed in 1970s feminist/hippie clothes.

Apart from the Prologue and Coda, the play is set in a multi-roomed Hollywood studio/sound stage in 1943. All action, imagined and real, takes place on the sound stage. Klieg lights, boom microphones, backdrops, and old set pieces litter the playing area.

The play's internal time is a single 24-hour period, perhaps a Wednesday.

Prologue

[Arzner sits at a table with a desk microphone before her. She is visibly in her late 40s, wearing a cardigan and a modest skirt, in contrast to her younger appearance later in the play. She is slightly stooped, with a beaten look. A voice-over announces her, followed by a lively 'theme music' jingle and a red light signalling that she is speaking 'On Air'. The voice-over is spoken by a male announcer with a clear, 1950s slick commercial style.]

VOICE-OVER: Westinghouse Radio Theatre and the new 1955 Cadillac Convertible – the automobile built for the future – proudly present *You Were Meant To Be a Star*, with your host, Hollywood motion picture director Miss Dorothy Arzner.

ARZNER: Good evening. Tonight's first letter is from a Miss Jane Gilbert of Pentachuta, Connecticut. *[reads letter]*

'Dear Miss Arzner, I am a college senior majoring in Library Science. I have been "pinned" to a senior boy in the pre-Medicine program for the last 17 months. We met on Valentine's Day – don't that beat all? He is tall and strong and kind and I'm positive he'll make a fine doctor some day. My problem is, when we both graduate next semester, he plans to attend a medical school in another state. I'm afraid his affections will wander. How do I get him to propose to me before it's too late?

P.S. If I may ask a personal question, why did you retire from your glamorous job as a top Hollywood director? It sounds just dreamy to me!'

In answer to your first question, Miss Gilbert, allow me to remind you that a woman is always at her most alluring when she recognizes a single, fundamental truth – all women are performers. During my career in motion pictures I made this my motto; and I continue to do so today, even in the more relaxed circumstances of radio broadcasting.

To be a woman is to be perpetually on stage. The saddest women today are those young ladies who forget to keep themselves quote 'camera ready' unquote. They are the lonely women one sees in bus shelters and all-night drugstores, drinking hopeful cup after hopeful cup of coffee and wondering why no one is paying them the slightest attention. Such women have forgotten their lines, their cues and their costumes. This simply will not do. My successful career as a provider of popular entertainments is entirely attributable to my ability to say without hesitation that I never once 'forgot my lines', so to speak.

My advice, Miss Gilbert, will be blunt. If you want your young doctor-to-be to become your husband-to-be, your path is clear – use every womanly tool at your disposal to shake him out of his complacency. My suspicion is that you have become old hat, more a buddy than a betrothed. A new dress, new shoes, a fresh hairstyle and a little powder are worth the price of a diamond ring on your finger. *[pause]*

In response to your second question, Miss Gilbert, the true reason I retired from Hollywood may forever remain a private matter, and I'd rather it did.

[Red 'On Air' light goes off. Arzner listens in growing darkness as Merle Oberon appears in a flickering light behind Arzner – Oberon's face is framed in a square of light, as if she were a projected film image. Oberon is a dazzling vision, accompanied by swelling, romantic movie music. Oberon speaks in a

projected, acting voice, delivering lines from a melodramatic film. Arzner remains seated with her back to the vision of Oberon, only hearing what the audience sees.]

OBERON: Who wants love? Who wants love? Who wants love? Love is a plaster pony ride at the circus. You spin and spin till you get so full of circles you forget your own name.

ARZNER: I spin and spin ... I wrote that line. Say it again.

OBERON: When the ponies cut to a grind, there you are – face a mess and stuck on some purple nag with green hair and a wild smile. Waiting. Waiting for some man to come along and help you down. You don't need his help. He knows it, you know it, but it's too late for logic.

ARZNER: My god, you hold the light. No line of your face is wasted. Merle Oberon, you were always good at stealing a scene. Of course, I taught you how. My god, you were so beautiful I sometimes forgot my own name. I wasted hours on your close-ups.

OBERON: I'm a husk, I'm a piece of arithmetic you've forgotten to calculate, forgot to figure. That's what love is, forgetting the details. You have to be a little bit blind and a whole lot dizzy. Who wants love? – sounds like influenza.

ARZNER: You can afford to be callous, Merle – the whole world still wants to touch you.

OBERON: You can touch me, pal. I'm only gold.

ARZNER: I still want to touch you.

VOICE-OVER: *[unheard by Arzner]* She's talking to herself again. Crazy old bulldog. She never 'forgets her lines' 'cause she never shuts the hell up. OK, here we go. *[to Arzner]* Miss Arzner, we're back in six seconds. Six, five, four, three ...

[Oberon vanishes, Arzner's red 'On Air' light returns. Arzner leaves table as rest of cast begins to assemble around her for Act One. They are clearly ghosts, characters of Arzner's memory and imagination.]

END

Act One

[Lights open on a Hollywood cafeteria, early in the morning. It is 1943. Harry Cohn and Louella Parsons sit at a table, smoking and talking. Rose Lindstrom and Oberon linger, apart, by a coffee urn. They whisper. Patriotic music from World War II plays quietly in the background.]

OBERON: Rose, have you read today's script pages?

LINDSTROM: Uh-huh.

OBERON: Well?

LINDSTROM: I thought we were making a war picture, but it says here I have to give you a big, um *[flips through script, reading]* 'compelling facial gesture of love and conviction'. Is that a kiss?

OBERON: It is not a handshake.

LINDSTROM: Is it legal?

OBERON: Certainly. In Mexico. Christ! Dorothy must be insane. Does she want the War Commission to put us all behind bars? There's a lesbian love scene for her.

LINDSTROM: *[reading script]* No kidding – you say to me: 'You spin and spin till you get so full of circles you forget your own name'. *[laughs]* You sound like a boy.

OBERON: After this, I'll be lucky if they let me tape down my breasts and do a submarine picture.

LINDSTROM: *[laughing and caressing Oberon's leg]* All hands on deck! All hands on deck!

OBERON: Sweetheart, submarines don't have decks. They go under the water ... *[sees Lindstrom's blank look]* ... never mind. *[lights cigarette]* No wonder Dorothy left this scene till the last day of filming – the studio is trapped, the money's already been spent.

LINDSTROM: *[tries to kiss Oberon]* Merle, don't you like to kiss me?

OBERON: *[pushes her away]* Idiot! Don't you like to eat?

LINDSTROM: Maybe this is a trick, a joke. She found out about you and me and she's jealous. She's showing her hand, but not for real – in a sneaky way. Kinda like playing poker.

OBERON: Do be quiet. I'm tired. I was up all night practicing my love scenes. *[sneaks a quick kiss, looks at script]* What can Dorothy be thinking? This scene was not part of the original script. I have a very firm contract and an even firmer lawyer –

LINDSTROM: Don't get riled yet. When we get to the set maybe we'll all just have a big laugh.

OBERON: *[holding Lindstrom's face]* Don't ever try to be sensible with me, my love, you'll upset my equilibrium.

LINDSTROM: *[sneaking a kiss]* I like your equilibrium, it's pretty. I dreamed about you last night. You and me, riding this big tank down Ventura Boulevard, and all the people were out on the streets cheering and throwing those paper bits –

OBERON: Confetti –

LINDSTROM: No, no food, just paper. Like pink snowflakes. *[becomes agitated]* And then this man jumps out of the crowd with a rifle in his hands –

OBERON: Rose, please. You're awake now. Have some coffee and clear your mind. One cup should do. *[points to Parsons]* She's as bright and bouncy as ever. I think I'll try hanging upside down at night.

LINDSTROM: Your face will fall. California has enough mudslides.

OBERON: And a surplus of starlets. Mind yourself.

LINDSTROM: You know, I wasn't born pretty, I willed it. I stared into the sun until all the ugly burned away. Nearly went blind. *[sneaks a second kiss]*

OBERON: *[brushing Lindstrom away]* See if you can will yourself over to another chair, I feel a little overexposed. *[prods Lindstrom along to a further chair]*

[Parsons and Cohn glance at Oberon and Lindstrom, watch the two women sit together at a distant table, then continue with their own whispered conversation.]

PARSONS: Where's Arzner?

COHN: I dunno.

PARSONS: Have you seen today's shooting script? Are you going to fire her? Can I watch?

COHN: Gheesh! Ain't there no immigrants or cripples you could kick around for fun? It's the last day of shooting. Sometimes Dorothy likes to make a little joke on the last day. She ain't crazy. She knows better than to make two girls go at it on film. It's gotta be a gag. I tell ya, Louella, Dorothy's always been a good girl for me.

PARSONS: How much money have you spent on this picture? Dorothy Arzner's war picture to inspire our brave boys at arms – a war picture with no male characters. It's a scandal.

COHN: Not yet it ain't. Keep your delicate little dictaphone off of Dorothy until it's official. There is a war on, Miss Chicago 1897.

PARSONS: Harry Cohn! You badger-bellied prick! Fortunately for you, I am constitutionally incapable of holding a grudge. And it's Miss Illinois, to be precise. Furthermore, I have never known a war yet that did not increase newspaper circulation. I like to think of all the boys overseas reading my little column, all a-dazzle about the goin's-on in Hollywood – who's kissing who, who's divorcing who, who's singing happy songs, who's crying in public, who's a worn-out bull dagger making war movies for deviants –

COHN: One word, one single word sees print and I'll sue your paper out of business!

PARSONS: You silly, where would you advertise your pictures?
[*both laugh*]

[*Lindstrom and Oberon catch laughter at the other table, watch for a moment, then continue to talk quietly.*]

LINDSTROM: [*flustered*] You oughta treat me nicer. Maybe I wasn't born with ballet slippers under my chin, but someday some part of me, a cheekbone or an ankle, someday someone's gonna see that perfect part of me and build a whole world around it. A world all about me – a new continent.

[*Arzner enters, unnoticed by Lindstrom. Arzner is a younger version of the woman seen in the prologue. She is dressed in a man's blazer and shirt and tie, with a long skirt. Her hair is slicked back and mannish. Oberon notices Arzner, and moves away from Lindstrom.*]

ARZNER: [*placing hand on Oberon's shoulder, looks over Lindstrom*] [*to Lindstrom*] When you find that special, undiscovered corner, polish it up – bring it around to me. [*to Oberon*] I like shiny things. Girlish things. [*to Lindstrom*] And I like my coffee black, and quick.

[*Arzner takes a seat next to Oberon, Lindstrom walks back to the coffee urn.*]

OBERON: You're causing quite a stir this morning.

ARZNER: [*caressing Oberon's arm*] You cause a stir all day long. Don't worry, everything will be fine.

OBERON: Careful, the Sphinx is watching.

ARZNER: She's old enough for the part. *[sneaking another caress]* Remember, I love you.

PARSONS: *[watching Arzner and Oberon]* I will live to be 102, and I am positive that even in my advanced age and abundant wisdom I shall never comprehend your reasoning for giving Dorothy Arzner a war picture. Dorothy simply does not understand – the camera is a man's eye.

ARZNER: *[hitting Oberon playfully with script]* What's the matter with you this morning – don't you like to kiss pretty girls?

OBERON: In the privacy of my own home. Or yours. *[pointing to Cohn]* He looks too calm.

ARZNER: All people with simple needs are calm. I can handle him, I've done it for years. I give him what he thinks he wants. *[pointing to Cohn's head]* You see, the motion picture camera is designed to draw a thin black line, a tiny telegraph cable, between the screen and the dumbest, most airless interiors of the American male psyche. And he's as thick as shoe leather.

OBERON: I dare you to say that a little louder.

ARZNER: I know Harry Cohn. He respects honesty.

OBERON: You told me once that the camera never lies.

ARZNER: Except when it's on.

PARSONS: *[to Cohn]* In fairness, however, Dorothy's hardly what anyone calls a woman.

COHN: Shut up, will ya? Dorothy's an old pro. She'll come through. Like I say, Dorothy has always been a good girl for me.

[Arzner raises her voice, Parsons, Cohn and Lindstrom all strain to listen.]

ARZNER: You don't understand ... my love ... it's *[kisses her furtively]* less than thirty seconds of screen time – twelve feet of film. Approximately the length of your bed. It's nothing. It's 720 frames, only five camera angles – one hour studio time – it will go by like lightning.

OBERON: I adore you, Dorothy, but you can't snow me with technicalities. My ideals go as far as the next actress – which is about the distance between here and the studio gates – but women do not kiss other women in pictures.

ARZNER: You sound like Harry. Merle, it's just 720 tiny little frames. You've got more diamonds than that. It's the blink of an eye. My eye. The camera makes you beautful, now I'll make you real.

OBERON: I've been real. I believe it was a Tuesday, in San Diego. Awfully rainy.

ARZNER: [takes Oberon's hand] I called you last night. Did you go out? I had a dream: we were on a ship together, surrounded by green waves. Suddenly, hundreds of flying fish came out of the water –

OBERON: Stop. Let's keep to the conscious world. There is a war on. We are expected to make useful, uplifting, deliciously worthless movies. Don't play games with my career over principles.

ARZNER: I'll film you in such a way that only me and the camera will understand.

OBERON: Then why bother? Why don't you just write me a poem? Flowers make a treat.

ARZNER: This is my love poem. Twenty feet high.

OBERON: You have no shame.

ARZNER: You have no courage.

OBERON: I'm still here, aren't I? Love, give the studio what it wants. Your integrity and these tits are already paid for.

ARZNER: *[laughs]* I adore you.

OBERON: Well quit it – nobody in this town is fireproof. Not me, not even you.

ARZNER: *[holding Oberon]* In big black type the screen will say 'A Dorothy Arzner Film'. That's right – a Dorothy Arzner film. Mine. And you're wrong, I am fireproof – I'm with you, aren't I?

PARSONS: *[to Cohn]* You'd be doing her a favour. Cut her off now and you can still finish the picture. Call in the script boys and make a new ending. You know how easy it is. Send her on vacation. The studio keeps a lovely little spa out in the desert. Lesbians like the desert, it's hard and scratchy. I'll do the story: 'Lady Director resigns from war picture due to kidney ailment'. Lesbians are always having kidney problems, due to the unnatural vacancy of their reproductive systems.

COHN: Ha! you don't got no kids – and far as I hear, your 'system' don't got no vacancies either.

PARSONS: Talk dirty all you like, but we both know making movies is not for the timid. A film is not a quilt, a film is a motorcar. Get in or get off the road.

COHN: One day, you're gonna push me too far.

PARSONS: Mr. Cohn, I am a daughter of the Midwest. We do not 'push', we encourage. Now call that aberration against femininity over here and show her what for!

ARZNER: Today, I have a chance to frame the film my way. An opportunity to make an honest picture.

OBERON: Pish! Any woman can get her chance, she's only got to look around.

ARZNER: It's not that simple for me. I'm not a movie star. I don't get to change between pictures. There is such a thing as 'A Dorothy Arzner Film' – it's my style, what people expect. Keeping my career is like sleeping with one eye open and one eye closed. But it protects me. And it's how you focus the lens. Like shooting a gun.

[Cohn waves Arzner and Oberon over.]

OBERON: [pushing Arzner away] Splendid idea: why don't you go volunteer for the front? I'll be a war bride – the public will love me. [rising to go to Cohn] He's calling. Mind you be sensible. See if you can keep both eyes open to reality for ten whole minutes.

[Lindstrom approaches Arzner's table with coffee for three, sees Arzner heading for Cohn's table and angrily follows Arzner and Oberon. All convene at Cohn's table.]

PARSONS: Dorothy! How nice. I was just completing the first paragraph of my column: 'In 1943 women starve to keep their children fed on food rations and Miss Dorothy Arzner makes feminine war pictures drenched in expensive silks and European ribbons'. Do you agree?

COHN: That's cute, go sell it to the Commie rags.

PARSONS: I personally feel sorry for any *artiste* who cannot grasp the fundamentals of popular morality. To be rejected by the public, to be set apart from one's fellow *artistes* – why, the isolation must be a devastation, a personal tragedy, like being sent out to the desert, the hard, scratchy desert –

COHN: Aw, let it alone, will ya? In America, glamour is more important than beans and sugar. Look at the Brits, one ugly war picture after the next. No offence, Oberon, but if I was a Brit and I hadda go to those movies I'd paint a target on my roof.

LINDSTROM: Did you hear about that actress in London, the one who cut off her dress right on the street during an air raid to make a bandage for a bleeding man? A bomb got her, split her clean in half. I'd like to be brave enough to do that, at least in a movie.

ARZNER: Unfortunately, in America, women are not asked to be brave, we are asked to be patient. *[to Cohn]* And obedient. Subsequently, there are only three roles for women in Hollywood: *[to Oberon]* maiden, *[to Cohn]* mother *[to Parsons]* and monster.

PARSONS: But Dorothy, director starts with a 'd'.

ARZNER: Keep going and you'll work your way up to full sentences.

COHN: *[to Lindstrom and Oberon] [whistles]* Ma and Pop are fighting. You kids beat it.

[Lindstrom and Oberon exit.]

ARZNER: *[to Parsons]* My movies make women move when the whole world tells women to sit still. And that makes you nervous.

PARSONS: Why, whatever do you mean? *[to Cohn]* But of course I acknowledge that I am out of my little puddle of intellectual depth. Thank goodness for brainful women like Dorothy. Every Hollywood coffee table needs at least one intellectual lesbian, don't you think?

ARZNER: Intellectual will do.

PARSONS: A lesbian anchors the room, sets the men at ease. More coffee, Dorothy?

ARZNER: So many poison cups, I've forgotten the taste.

PARSONS: You have no taste. Being, as it is, part and parcel of decorum.

ARZNER: As is serving your guests. *[holds cup out to Parsons]*

COHN: Now, now, ladies, make nice. Dorothy don't like scenes.

ARZNER: But I like you.

PARSONS: You two make a smart pair – all business. It's so refreshing. But anything unnatural is, for a short time.

COHN: Hell right I'm all business. I talk business at lunch, I talk business at dinner. I talk business in my sleep. *[motions to Parsons to leave him alone with Arzner, Parsons gets up for more coffee]* Shit, Dotty, I even talk business on the privy.

ARZNER: So, let's talk business. I've got one day left on this film, and I like to finish a picture on time. You've read today's script?

COHN: You can't hear my ulcers screaming?

ARZNER: It reads worse than it looks.

COHN: Tell to me please when I have ever interfered in your work? Tell me the one time I've done such a thing? Never. So maybe for once you can do something for me. No kissing between girls.

ARZNER: Look at the context of the whole movie – it fits.

COHN: Like a knife in my back.

ARZNER: All I'm asking for is the same control over my pictures you give other directors. If I was a man I'd –

PARSONS: *[re-entering conversation]* Dorothy, good heavens. If you were any more of a man you'd be safely off to war. Perhaps in the deserts of Egypt –

COHN: *[to Parsons]* Enough already!

PARSONS: Dorothy, I dislike aggressiveness in women. I like it even less in you. *[rises to exit, to Cohn]* Duty beckons. I have a deadline to meet – we'll talk later?

ARZNER: And sooner. And all the damned time in between.

[*Parsons exits.*]

COHN: Dorothy, try to be nice. She don't mean no real harm. She's just curious. I think maybe she really likes you. We all like you. Everyone just wants what's best. This picture, what is it? It's one movie. One movie you can finish by dinner and move on. Finish today, end the picture like me who loves you is telling you to do, which is not with girls kissing girls, and I promise I'll give you a new picture to make. A good romance. We'll do it in New England, lots of snow scenes, huh?

ARZNER: It's all so easy for you. You've never made a picture. Your name's not on the poster. Harry, we've been friends a long time.

COHN: Look, Dot, friends is nice but this is money. Don't abuse my affections. Now and then I turn bad.

ARZNER: I could hardly trust you if you didn't. And I do trust you, most of the time.

COHN: Look, your movie's got some good stuff, stuff I like. Nice-looking women, the war angle. It's a little highbrow maybe – I mean, it's hard enough selling the trash these days.

ARZNER: But?

COHN: Dot, you and me got no secrets. I know you – you fall in love with these girls and suddenly you gotta do another big social issue picture. And what happens? No ticket sales and more innuendo in the scandal sheets. You directors is all alike – you wanna schtup the leading lady. Fine, be my guest. But have some dignity.

ARZNER: You cheapen the situation.

COHN: No, you do, with all this indiscretion. I like Merle, she's got kick. [elbows Arzner] Huh? Huh? But stop advertising – the world will catch you.

ARZNER: [exasperated] That's my business.

COHN: Not when you wanna put it on the screen. Dotty, there's an awful amount of talk.

ARZNER: I don't listen to Louella.

COHN: Good for you, but everybody reads the papers. Dot, you and me know there's a million ways to end a movie, but if the public sees you with Merle and then they see Merle making mush with another broad on the screen, they'll put two and two together and get three to five in Sing Sing.

Why don't we marry you off to one of the faggots in wardrobe, then you can make all the lesbo pictures you want?

The audience, see, they know already about the girls in your picture – but they don't wanna be told outright 'cause then there's evidence and people prefer to know dirty things inside their heads. It makes them feel smart. The heart don't need eyes.

ARZNER: It's only one kiss. Women kiss all the time. Why are Americans incapable of imagining women in love? I'm giving the audience psychology ... a whole continent, built on a single, perfect face. Merle's face. Look at the rest of the picture – women in airplanes, spies, murder, heroism.

Nobody will even imagine –

COHN: Perverts? To you I say this: say what? And so what? If this big continent on Merle's face is so blinding nobody's gonna notice she's making hooey with cutie face, what's your point? Is it a lesbo picture or not a lesbo picture?

ARZNER: Both. It depends on who's watching.

COHN: Oh no, don't try that on me. Don't give me such *tsuros* to make a lesbo picture nobody's gonna know is a lesbo picture. And if they do figure it out, it's now a picture I can't show. This is logic?

Me, I'm practical. I say let the Krauts make the art pictures, that's how they lost the last war. I gotta tell ya I hate art pictures anyway. My father, god rest his bastard soul, he used to swear every movie he ever saw was about balls: 'Think balls. Who's got balls, who don't. Throw in a conflict, you got drama'.

ARZNER: You don't believe what you're saying. We've made good movies together, movies that changed things. Now I want more. I want to make movies about things I can't mention in polite society. All my secrets, twenty feet high. The eyes teach the heart – we feel what we see – and you taught me that.

COHN: That's very pretty but still I say thank you no. Dotty, I love you like my own brother, but lately your films are not paying. And now you wanna make pervert history? Your movies are like poetry – they're pretty, they make the heart soar. I got no problem with any of that except it don't make money.

ARZNER: Take the losses out of my percentage.

COHN: [sighs] This town is full of lesbos and I gotta sign the one who wants to direct. Go into costumes like the other daggers.

ARZNER: I know what I'm doing. [puts one hand over Cohn's left eye] This is how the camera works – one eye shut dark, one eye wide as a summerhouse gate. Voluntary blindness.

COHN: And from this demonstration I am deducing what?

ARZNER: The audience can only see what it wants to see. It's built into the camera. Voluntary blindness.

COHN: [gets up to leave] Try putting that on the poster.
    You want to make dirty movies, fine. I'll set you up in the back lot. All the girls you need. But don't ask me to put my family name behind a secret-code movie that only deviates and the censor board can figure out.

ARZNER: [stands up, covers Cohn's eyes with hands] Can you see me? [lifts one hand off his face] How about now?

COHN: Sure, I can see you OK.

ARZNER: [takes second hand off] Better?

COHN: Dotty ...

ARZNER: I've spent my whole life in half light, one blink away from disappearing. I'm afraid it's permanent.

COHN: Dotty, you gotta calm down.

ARZNER: Whoever blinks first loses.

COHN: One scene, Dotty. That's all I ask.

ARZNER: Last night when the set was dark I looked into the lens ... the black doubled back on me. I saw my own eye reflected in the focus. My eye was shaking, I was shaking. Like a trapped cat. [laughs] I've made too many films to be so skittish.

COHN: Dot ... Dotty, think it out. Two times in your life you're gonna feel secure – when you got a big hit and when you're dead, and you never had a big hit yet.

ARZNER: That hurts, Harry.

COHN: [pauses] How about the two girls make with a really long hug? Huh?

ARZNER: Sure ... fine. I'll just shut my eyes.

COHN: There we go – everybody's friends again. Be a good girl.

   END

Act Two

*[Arzner paces before a camera. Lindstrom and Oberon rehearse
a kiss scene over and over. They are dressed in military costume.]*

ARZNER: *[bending to look in her lens]* No, higher. I can see up
Miss Oberon's nose. Stop. *[to Lindstrom]* Take your bottom
lip, pull it out – no, like this *[she demonstrates]* – and glide
the inside of your lip just under the bottom of her lip –
no, no. Miss Lindstrom, would you come here please?
[motions Lindstrom over] Do as I do. *[demonstrates kiss on
Lindstrom]*

LINDSTROM: You'll pardon me, Miss Arzner, but I've been
kissed better by horses.

ARZNER: *[guiding Lindstrom to view scene through camera lens]*
Watch. *[approaches Oberon, gives her a long, passionate kiss
while Lindstrom watches]* A kiss that feels good ... rarely
looks good.

OBERON: *[flustered]* It's like buying shoes.

ARZNER: Let's take five minutes, shall we? *[into megaphone]*
Five-minute break!

[Lindstrom exits.]

OBERON: What did Cohn say?

ARZNER: *[unbuttoning Oberon's blouse]* Shhh. Not now. Not
now.

OBERON: When?

ARZNER: You're shaking ...

OBERON: I suspect I like you too much.

ARZNER: [nuzzling Oberon] Courage, courage.

OBERON: What did Cohn tell you?

ARZNER: Harry told me I should take you behind the prop house and – [whispers rest into her ear]

OBERON: Now that I believe!

ARZNER: [places Oberon on her lap] Hmmm ... I want a whole face of kisses.

OBERON: [unbuttons her blouse, offers Arzner her breasts] Are you sure no one is watching?

ARZNER: [laughing, fondling] You're cute when you're demure.

OBERON: I'm cute all the time. Dorothy, tell me what Cohn said ... annnnnd I'll kiss the pink parts inside you. I'll go so deep you'll need a rope to pull me back.

ARZNER: [kissing Oberon's face] Hmmm ... I love a good magic trick. [turns camera on Merle as they kiss] Just relax, be natural.

OBERON: [sees camera is on] Jesus Christ! Turn that cursed thing off!

ARZNER: [pulls away] Shhh!

OBERON: [pushes away, buttons up blouse clumsily] Really, darling, you know my motto – natural acting is neither. What a nerve you've got.

ARZNER: I seem to do better with women this big. *[makes a small square with her fingers]* Sorry, bad habit.

OBERON: You are an odd creature.

ARZNER: You're so beautiful – *[laughs]* when I'm with you I have to prove I'm real.

[Arzner tries to kiss and film Oberon again.]

OBERON: *[pushing Arzner away]* You're real enough. Real trouble. *[fusses with blouse]* Oh, hell, look at me now ... what did Harry tell you?

ARZNER: *[angry, shuts off camera]* Forget it. *[into megaphone]* Let's get back to work, people!

[Lindstrom returns, both stand before a white screen. Arzner faces them with a camera. Lindstrom's face is traced by a blunt square of white light. Cohn enters, paces behind Arzner, anxiously watching the film shoot.]

ARZNER: Please turn to the left, I need to check the light levels. Now the right, please. Thank you. Any time you feel ready ... Action!

[Lindstrom and Oberon silently act out their kissing scene.]

COHN: *[watching the scene]* Dorothy, you're ruining me! What am I gonna tell the Catholic League for Decency? Today I produced a nice little patriotic film about two bull daggers whoring around the fields of France killing Nazis. Cut!

ARZNER: Cut! Get me a longer boom, and sharpen the focus on Miss Oberon's torso. Can we try to reduce the shine on Miss Lindstrom's shoulders? Thank you. [whispers to Cohn] You are undermining my authority on the set.

COHN: You're goddamn right I'm undermining your authority – I'm gonna bazooka your authority! Are you crazy?

ARZNER: You don't understand feminine behaviour.

COHN: Fine, then please translate for me – do girls always kiss each other full on the mouth before they shoot Nazi collaborators? How come they don't do that in westerns?

ARZNER: Well, these women are Europeans. [to Lindstrom and Oberon] Let's try the scene again, please. Miss Oberon, if you could place your left leg under your backside – no, the knee should be more pronounced. [drags a boom mike over the scene] Let's have a sound check please, Miss Lindstrom.

LINDSTROM: [acting scene, badly] That's right, I said die – die because I love you –

ARZNER: Thank you. [moves microphone] Again. [Lindstrom says line again, or shorter version of same] Stop. Perfect. [frames shot with a pocket lens] Miss Oberon, the knee? Silence please ... Action!

LINDSTROM: [acting scene with Oberon] That's right, I said die – die because I love you. Remember me when the axe falls, remember that I love you. I'll swing for you, but I'll take the rope in both my hands and whisper your name.

COHN: Get me the script girl! Script girl, I said!

ARZNER: Cut! I need silence! Harry, it's your money being wasted.

LINDSTROM: Sorry. Was I outside my light again?

ARZNER: No, Mr. Cohn was inside my ear. Take a few minutes and fix up your faces. [paces] Maybe the point of view is wrong. [to Cohn] What do you think – speech, responding shot, speech or speech, speech, speech and then responding shot?

COHN: [wiping face with handkerchief] Here's a responding shot – I come in from behind the trees dressed like a Kraut and shoot the both of them dead. A perfectly noble ending!

OBERON: Mr. Cohn, let's all settle down, shall we? Would you like some brandy? [snaps fingers at Lindstrom to get Cohn a drink; Lindstrom brings him a shot, he drinks it] Now, we're all adults here. You have to forgive Dorothy – she's Californian, she sometimes forgets to drive the speed limit.

COHN: [puts down glass calmly] Don't smooth talk with me, Oberon. I'll eat your contract myself and shit it down your throat.

LINDSTROM: Am I gonna have to learn new lines?

OBERON: Now Harry, you know how I adore you. I love you so much that when I die I want my ashes spread across your driveway so your car won't skid.

COHN: I doubt your corpse will burn so good. *[wiping face]* Dotty, listen to me one minute – for a war picture I'm telling you gotta give me something more conventional.

ARZNER: You mean more dishonest.

COHN: More like legal.

ARZNER: If you'd only let me show you what I intend –

COHN: Shut up with that – you think maybe I'm stupid? Don't forget who signs the cheques, Arzner. I've burned films before. They glow real pretty, all blue like.

[Parsons enters, carrying a lunch bag.]

COHN: Oh joy. Hey, ace reporter, where's my blindfold and last cigarette?

PARSONS: My dear, all you ever have to do is ask.

ARZNER: Places, ladies.

COHN: I'm gonna sit in my office for one hour and dream of a nice quick stroke. Then I'm coming back, and everything will be just the way I want it. Or else I get ugly.

[Cohn exits. Oberon and Lindstrom reassemble on the set, trying to catch the conversation between Parsons and Arzner.]

PARSONS: I like the way Harry explodes. Like a Mexican birthday party. Have you ever seen a woman ball up her fists like that? No. Men smash, women cut. I prefer the smash – so much more direct than journalism.

ARZNER: *[resets her camera while Oberon and Lindstrom wait for directions]* You'll forgive me if I work.

PARSONS: We're all working today, Dorothy. *[tries to peek into Arzner's camera]* People say you have the tightest mouth in Hollywood. People say you wouldn't yell fire in Hades.

ARZNER: I have a fear of redundancy, and newspapers. It amounts to the same thing.

PARSONS: *[with pencil and notepad]* What is this final scene about, Dorothy? Don't you trust me?

ARZNER: This film is about focusing and refocusing. Long shots and close-ups. This is a film about costumes and makeup and backlighting and set design and sound levels.
I wish they'd lock the doors around here.

PARSONS: Be careful, Dorothy, nobody in America roots for the clever girl.

ARZNER: Then I am a failure as an American. I root for the clever girl. I guess it's a psychological block, but it makes me happy.

PARSONS: Now we are flying with the birds. Psychology! No filth blows out my umbrella more briskly than psychology! Let's you and I share an honest moment – you dress like a baseball player and you make movies about confused women in long silver dresses. Where the hell were you brought up?

ARZNER: This is a film about high contrasts. You see, in this scene I'm using very high-powered lights [points to Parsons's face] to bleach out crow's feet, shadows under the eyes. Like most pictures, this is a film about hairdressing and set decorating and props.

PARSONS: Do I appear to be without the blessing of hearing? Am I speaking Spanish? You are too smart for my own good: talk to me, buttercream, before somebody else does. I need an angle for this story by this afternoon – make sense now, before Harry takes all your pretty girls away.

ARZNER: This is a film about ... two women bonding together during a time of international conflict.

PARSONS: Try again, loverboy.

[Oberon and Lindstrom giggle nervously.]

ARZNER: [to Parsons] Damn you! Get off my set!

PARSONS: Dorothy, heavens! Such language.

[Arzner swings the boom mike over Parsons' head and shoves the microphone aggressively into Parsons' face.]

ARZNER: [takes boom mike in hand] I invented this. The boom mike. My idea. Watch any talkie from '31 or '32. You're old enough to remember – nobody moves. All the actors are like chess pieces, frozen, waiting for their square to open up. Like you. I changed all that – I let actors use their legs. The same way I'm going to liberate you.

PARSONS: Don't you dare lay a hand on me!

ARZNER: *[laughing]* Look at you, you're frozen. Frozen in old stories and ancient scandals and the entire history of sexual intercourse in Southern California since 1900. You're cornered. *[takes Parsons by the arm]*

PARSONS: *[prepares to defend herself]* Miss Arzner, you are taxing my composure!

ARZNER: Here's your chance to get out, here's your chance to write a real story, here's your ticket out from under the mattresses of teenage girls – you have one chance to ask me one singularly adult, intelligent and useful question about the art of filmmaking.

PARSONS: *[into the microphone]* Is it true Miss Oberon promised to do three pictures for free just to get out of this one?

OBERON: Really! The only people I allow to lie to my face are royalty.

[Oberon exits in anger. Arzner turns the boom away from Parsons' face, defeated.]

PARSONS: *[looks into lens of Arzner's camera]* Am I in there too? Am I allowed in your privileged, highbrow world? I am a woman too – why else would I watch?

ARZNER: *[shoves Parsons away from camera]* This is my film, my eye ... you'll watch, you always watch. You're drawn to the light.

PARSONS: Finish your thought, Dorothy. For once in your life finish an honest, clean sentence. It'll set you free.

ARZNER: If I give you an honest answer, one of us will disappear.

PARSONS: Shit on Sunday, Dorothy, I'll say it for you: this is a film about two girls fucking. Any poor fool can see that, and this poor fool can print it.

[Parsons exits.]

ARZNER: *[to Lindstrom]* Clear the set!

[Lindstrom exits. Arzner is left alone. She focuses and refocuses the camera obsessively, plays with the lights and microphones, paces.]

ARZNER: Nothing pleases them. Nothing. All these years, making movies to please people who don't know what they want. I'm tired of it.

Make it sexier, Dorothy. Dorothy, that's too racy. Your female characters are too mean, Dorothy. Dorothy, why don't you give these girls some spunk? That's an odd camera angle, Dorothy, I can't see her tits. Dorothy, you've got your camera down her top. Dorothy, you're too highbrow. Dorothy, you are simplifying the story. Your films are too cold. Whoa, Dorothy, turn the heat down. Dorothy, your films are so poetic. Dorothy, if people want poetry, they buy a book.

DAMN DAMN DAMN

Nothing is ever enough, ever just right ... I have spent my entire career giving the least possible intellectual content to the most educated audience in the history of the world. All I've got, everything inside me, I have given to people who can't remember the title of my films ten minutes after the credits. *[pause]*

Not this time. One kiss. One kiss will forgive all the lies, clear off all the mud, the years and years of saying yes and meaning I hate you. One kiss will complete my open, cloudless blue sky of a movie. No winks, no layers, no hidden stories, no secret signals. One perfect, true film and I can start over. I can make honest movies, honest movies for discerning, mature audiences.

One kiss, and this film is mine.

END

Act Three

[Parsons and Cohn meet.]

COHN: You look disappointed. No news for you is good news for me.

PARSONS: Now, be nice. Everyone else is these days. Nice and quiet. Are you going to let her film two women kissing?

COHN: What you saw today was nothing but a little womanly comraderie.

PARSONS: What I saw was a well–oiled deviant machine.

COHN: *[sighs]* Here we go.

PARSONS: This whole town moves like a well–oiled machine. But I prefer to peek underneath the axle, see what the road brought home. Might be a flower from the ditch, might be a dead cat. Flowers make good back pages, but dead cats pay the bills.

COHN: And make a swell lunch.

PARSONS: Smart aleck! Are you going to fire Dorothy? I have a two o'clock deadline, and I need a fat, dead cat.

COHN: Damn dirty work.

PARSONS: You're getting soft where you sit. I declare – the nerve of that woman! I detest career women, they jar the natural order of life.

COHN: You got a career.

PARSONS: I understand my place. I am not an adventuress.

COHN: Sweetheart, how long we all known each other? Thirty years? I knew Dorothy when we was all kids. To be honest with you, I never thought she'd make it past editing. Boy, could she edit – like cutting paper dolls. Then Paramount signs her to direct. I figure it's a stunt, like girls trying to swim the English Channel. So I'm wrong. A dozen pictures later I'm still wrong. You gotta respect that.

PARSONS: A dozen movies and not one of them worth a damn to watch.

COHN: Aw, let it go. Your problem is you don't like women as smart as you.

PARSONS: Women like Dorothy give other women dangerous ideas. She frightens people.

COHN: And you I suppose make little children feel safe at night.

PARSONS: [pause] I have played by the rules all of my life. I have made my sacrifices and looked the other way to obey those rules and I have been handsomely rewarded. But the rules are not written by women. Who the hell is Dorothy Arzner to set herself above the rest of us?

COHN: Rules is rules, true, and you've put your time in – but now you're so high up in the tower you forget people ain't really midgets.

PARSONS: Are you going to make Dorothy bend?

COHN: Dorothy will do as she's told.

PARSONS: Why do you protect Dorothy at my expense? Directors come and go, but I am eternal. You forget who your friends are. *[Parsons begins to exit]*

COHN: *[nervous]* I forget nothing. It's my curse. You are my friend, Dorothy is my friend. Don't ask for me to choose.

PARSONS: When I started in this business, I used to think honest people with honest jobs treated each other better. But I was wrong. Everybody talks.
    Americans have erased the animal urge for self-preservation, but something's missing. What is it? Information: the last American appetite.

COHN: *[squeezes her]* Not quite. Come home with me tonight.

PARSONS: Angel cake, you insult my journalistic integrity. Which home?

COHN: It's nice and quiet up in the hills.

PARSONS: Hmm, closer to heaven. Come pick me up later, after you speak to Dorothy. I'd prefer to watch fireworks from a distance. Treat me nice, and my typewriter is very co-operative.

COHN: Like a well–oiled machine.

[Arzner and Oberon, in a back room.]

ARZNER: You look so good with Rose. Perfect composition. Beautiful.

OBERON: I don't suppose you noticed all the screaming?

ARZNER: I don't notice much when you're around.

OBERON: Remind me not to cross the street with you.

ARZNER: Do you like Rose? Do you think she's pretty?

OBERON: You cast her.

ARZNER: No, I mean, in real life.

OBERON: There's a first ... Rose is a lovely girl. You know that.

ARZNER: What else is she?

OBERON: A Republican? Really, Dorothy, I don't understand the question.

ARZNER: What else is she to you?

OBERON: An actress.

ARZNER: You two, you look so perfect together. You radiate.

OBERON: [kissing Arzner] Don't be jealous of your own creation. You'll go mad.

ARZNER: [pulls away] What did I create?

OBERON: A scene, Dorothy, a momentary episode. A fiction. 720 tiny little frames. It will all pass by in a lightning blink – remember?

ARZNER: [kissing Oberon] I'm sorry. Sometimes I get so confused.

OBERON: Then close your eyes. [attempts to kiss Arzner]

ARZNER: [ignoring Oberon's kiss] I'll see you on the set.

[Cohn and Lindstrom meet in a hallway.]

COHN: Oh, it's you.

LINDSTROM: That's what everyone says to me.

COHN: What a mess, huh?

LINDSTROM: Funny, that's the second thing everybody always says.

COHN: Listen, I gotta ask – does it bother you when Dorothy says to do what she wants you to do?

LINDSTROM: It's called directing, sir.

COHN: No, no. I mean, this kiss business.

LINDSTROM: Oh. Sure, a little. It feels sorta dirty. But most of the parts I get feel sorta dirty anyway.

COHN: Honey, listen – what is your name again?

LINDSTROM: Rose. Rose, Rose, Rose: I'm the girl nobody knows.

COHN: Sure, Rose. OK, honey, listen – it occurs to me maybe you and me got related problems.

LINDSTROM: I was brought up to be helpful, Mr. Cohn.

COHN: I seen you with Oberon, she throws you looks you could pour on waffles.

LINDSTROM: Tell me what you want, Mr. Cohn.

COHN: My dilemma is, I give Dorothy the heave from this picture, I don't look so good. You see, I stuck up for her with the money people. You know what they're like, million-dollar houses and dime-store brains – they get scared easy. I can't stand for somebody to say I told you so.

LINDSTROM: I want better parts.

COHN: Say again?

LINDSTROM: First I want to do a Tarzan picture, so folks can see my figure. Then I want to die in a picture, slowly, so folks will see me act. Then I want to play a girl gone bad, a whore type – it increases my award potential.

COHN: [holds Lindstrom's face] You got good bones. Good for close-ups. [grabs her by the waist] Oberon don't always listen so good.

LINDSTROM: I should do a musical after the whore part. So the public doesn't get the wrong idea. I've got a voice like a church bell.

COHN: You got a deal. Now, go sing for it.

[Lindstrom and Oberon by a makeup table, Oberon is staring at her own reflection.]

LINDSTROM: You look all in. Is it your time?

OBERON: *[distracted]* Time?

LINDSTROM: I can hardly think at all during my days. It's the only time a girl is left to herself. I make a lot of demands, usually confused.

OBERON: May I suggest you've discovered the title of your autobiography – 'Usually Confused'. Can you leave me alone for a while?

LINDSTROM: I get terrible muddled. It helps to get good and drunk. Clears my head.

OBERON: If you started walking right now, how long do you suppose it would take you to go to hell?

LINDSTROM: Jeez, you're awful mean.

OBERON: It happens when your career turns to shit. Just wait.

LINDSTROM: Dorothy's got you under a spell. I seen it before, with lotsa girls. You're just her blank slate. Better run before you get erased.

OBERON: Why must you constantly speak in metaphor? It's like talking to a socialist.

LINDSTROM: You're not her first.

OBERON: If you don't shut up –

LINDSTROM: She'll wreck your life. She can't help it. But I can.

OBERON: So, be helpful. [takes Lindstrom in a rough kiss]

[Parsons enters.]

PARSONS: Between us gals, you two are swaddling a dark secret. I'll get to it, I always do. I need merely close my eyes and think dreadful, black thoughts and something unmentionable always comes to me.

LINDSTROM: There's no story here for you. I learned once in school about people like you – conquistadors. They went in ships to the edge of the world, and the first thing at the end of the ocean was always a sea monster – nobody saw a chorus of angels or a marble palace, or anything beautiful or good. Just the same old monsters. Guarding the door to nothing. Kinda sad, huh? [wanders off]

PARSONS: Well! I am certain I do not know what all that is supposed to mean!

But let us maintain the nautical allusions – Merle Oberon, you are bobbing in some very high waves. Fortunately, you intrigue me.

May I safely propose, meaning no offense, that you have never been an American star? Why is it so many fine English actors fail to land securely on Hollywood soil?

OBERON: We can act.

PARSONS: *[laughs]* True, true. And irrelevant. Publicity, blossom, publicity is the answer. Think of me as a lighthouse, shining your path to the front page. The headline is up to you.

OBERON: I'm tired of swimming.

PARSONS: We all swim together here, Miss Oberon. One little storm on the beach, and all our pretty houses get blown away. You and Arzner are disrupting the tides. Cut Dorothy off, bring that woman to heel, and I will make you a real star – an American star. Save yourself, the water's rising.

OBERON: Women and children and traitors first, is it?

PARSONS: *[laughs]* Child! That only happens in the movies. Do you want to be courageous or play courageous?

OBERON: *[pauses, considers]* How big a star?

PARSONS: Take my hand, and we'll eclipse the sun.

OBERON: I love America.

PARSONS: Prove it. *[holds out her hand, Oberon reluctantly shakes it]*

END

Act Four

[Lindstrom enters, finding the set empty. Arzner enters.]

ARZNER: I apologize for the delays. Where is Merle?

LINDSTROM: It's a mutiny.

ARZNER: Never mind. Let's rehearse your lines, shall we?

LINDSTROM: *[performing scene]* When you come to me tonight I won't be afraid. If I'm a stone, let me sink.

ARZNER: Stop, stop there. May I ask you a personal question? Have you ever been in love?

LINDSTROM: Uh–huh. The first year I came to town. Some, uh, producer. He, uh, he helped me. I got a lot of auditions. I tested for Anne Boleyn – too tall. I tested for Salome – too skinny. That's my story: my head's too big, my eyes are too small, my legs are too short. I was born in the wrong century.

ARZNER: No, no, don't ever say that. There is no right century for a woman.

LINDSTROM: I've been in nine pictures and three serials but nobody knows my name. Sometimes I think I was meant to be filmed, not talked to.

ARZNER: Nonsense. Let's try those lines again. Say the lines to me and put that producer's face over mine. See him.

LINDSTROM: *[performing]* I'll take life, take it in the teeth like a bullet. Pain's the one thing nobody wants to steal.

ARZNER: Much better.

LINDSTROM: Miss Arzner, I'm afraid you're never going to work again after this picture.

ARZNER: More mutiny?

LINDSTROM: I had a dream last night. I was drowning in Jack Warner's pool. This little orange cat came up to the side of the pool and started licking his tail, watching me go down three times. It wasn't a devil cat, it just didn't know no better … Like you. You just don't know no better. But people get hurt. People who can't swim.

ARZNER: Anyone can swim. It's a natural animal reflex. Drowning is the result of panic. People drown themselves. The human body is naturally floatative. One need only lie flat and –

LINDSTROM: Wait?

ARZNER: Breathe. Good things come to actors who wait.

LINDSTROM: Do you believe that?

ARZNER: Yes, entirely.

LINDSTROM: What about people, real people I mean?

ARZNER: I don't see the difference.

LINDSTROM: Well, I do! You see, my mother says I got one more year here in Hollywood and then if I don't make it big I gotta come home and get married. Back to Mayflower, Arizona – nothing but men that smell like rust and Indians and lost women.

ARZNER: There are no lost women, only women who've forgotten their scripts.

LINDSTROM: I like you, you talk to me like I'm smart. How come you don't talk to Merle like you do me?

ARZNER: You understand Merle, don't you?

LINDSTROM: Sure. Well, most of the time. She yells a lot.

ARZNER: Merle yells when she's scared. Or in love.

LINDSTROM: [evasively] I wouldn't know nothing about that.

ARZNER: [laughing] You lie much more effectively on film.

LINDSTROM: I think I have to go to the bathroom.

ARZNER: Take Merle, she's yours.

LINDSTROM: Ain't that kinda up to her?

ARZNER: Merle doesn't know what she wants – Merle has to be shown what she wants. She's like a child. I'll give her to you. Bring her here, finish my film with my ending, and I'll show Merle how much she wants you.

LINDSTROM: You make me cold inside.

ARZNER: Do we understand each other?

LINDSTROM: Miss Arzner, you got this last scene all worked out for yourself but I don't like to set people against me.

[Cohn enters, unseen.]

ARZNER: I'm offering you a chance to make history.

LINDSTROM: Look, I'm not ashamed ... I've got secrets, everybody does ... things I'm not proud of but I did anyway. But you and me are different, you got control. With me, it's just that sometimes I'm the cat and sometimes I'm floating in the pool.

ARZNER: Don't let yourself drown.

[A bright light bears down on Arzner and Lindstrom. Cohn stands behind the pedestal holding the light.]

ARZNER: [*squinting agaist light*] Turn that off, please. Who is it?

COHN: Dot, we got business. Get rid of her.

LINDSTROM: Hello, Mr. Cohn.

COHN: Get out already!

[*Lindstrom exits.*]

ARZNER: What the hell is so important? I have a film to finish.

COHN: You made me a promise. Louella is hanging over me like a noose.

ARZNER: Turn that damned light off.

COHN: Oh, no no – I want to see your pretty face up close when you tell me how happy you are to do whatever I ask. Humour me.

ARZNER: [*stands by the screen, Cohn trails her with light*] This is beneath you.

COHN: Let's try a scene, you and me. Let's me and you do the scene where you decide to change the ending of this smutty little movie.

ARZNER: It is not a smutty little anything. I'm not responsible for your ignorance.

COHN: I don't give a Siamese fuck. You, however, have pulled on my pant leg for the last time. Do as I tell you.

ARZNER: It's my film.

COHN: No, it's mine. I paid for it. And a funny thing about movies that cost money – suddenly I don't care a dog's ass for artistic vision: I have a product to sell and it's your job to fix it. Do your job. Do as I tell you.

ARZNER: I am the director.

COHN: A director's job, Dorothy, is to make shiny pictures for the men who pay for them. I like shiny pictures. Everybody I know likes shiny pictures. Shiny, clean, safe pictures.
 You will do as I tell you or I will find someone else who can. [stands up] I'll see you at the rushes.

[Cohn exits.]

ARZNER: My rushes ... my film.

[Oberon enters, wearing a hooded dress.]

OBERON: Dorothy, you're asking too much.

ARZNER: Like everyone else today ... I'm asking you to walk the plank.

OBERON: Good god! Walk the plank?

ARZNER: It's a game I played when I was a girl, a summer game. One girl stands at the end of the wharf, the other girl walks down to the water, blindfolded. The girl at the end of the wharf keeps telling her to walk, but the blindfolded girl only stops when she thinks she's just about to go over. It's a trust game.

OBERON: Why doesn't the girl with the blindfold just peek?

ARZNER: Because she wants to fall in.

OBERON: So, she never actually wins the game?

ARZNER: The worst thing that can happen is she gets dunked in the lake, and that's exactly what she wants to begin with. She can always open her eyes in the air, before the splash.
    I want you to jump.

OBERON: You're too late. It's too late. We had our fun … you're sweet, Dorothy, in a brainy sort of way … but now it's too complicated. You turn on that camera, and I have to start thinking about my future.

ARZNER: I'm offering you a chance to make the future. I'm offering you a place in history. Walk the plank. Somebody has to get wet.

OBERON: The only place I'm getting wet is in my beautiful new pool in my beautiful new home decorated with my beautiful new furniture –

[Arzner walks off.]

OBERON: Dorothy, come back – I'm sorry, I'm sorry. I do understand falling. It's just that I fall … and you get to watch. That's not fair. It's my face on the screen, not yours.

ARZNER: Poor little Merle, spoiled by the spotlight. Don't be another stupid actor – you'll be forgotten in ten years.

OBERON: Not if I'm careful.

ARZNER: The water's warm, Merle. Walk the plank.

OBERON: No.

ARZNER: A few seconds, Merle. Heartbeats. Pretend you're with me.

OBERON: NO Dorothy, NO. My god, you're exasperating!
[pause]
　　I can't stand it any longer. You've had the real Merle in your bed, be satisfied.

ARZNER: I love you. I'm not going to live in halves anymore. You understand, don't you?

OBERON: I understand you've got a film with no ending, or an ending no one will ever see. [laughs] Really, I think this situation makes you happy: it's rather like the way you fuck – no payoff.
　　Throw yourself to the wolves if you want. There is a entire city out there full of disappointed people just waiting, waiting for me to ruin myself. I won't do it!

[Lindstrom enters. Arzner grabs both women, forcing them to enact the kiss scene while she arranges her camera.]

ARZNER: You'll do it for her.

OBERON: You listen to me, Dorothy – I am going to survive you. The same way she'll survive me, and you'll survive till your next picture comes along.

ARZNER: [laughing] There are no lost women.

OBERON: Stop this, you're hurting me.

ARZNER: [laughing] Do you know what Edison called the camera? The Lying Machine. The Lying Machine, Merle, the Lying Machine!

OBERON: Please, Dorothy, please. You're not well. Listen, we'll do another picture. [takes Arzner's hand] Please, please –

LINDSTROM: Merle, it don't matter now. She can't tell the difference … C'mon. [takes Oberon in her arms, prepares for kiss]

ARZNER: [positions camera, films scene] Places please! Ladies … Action!

[Lindstrom and Oberon enact the final kiss scene for Arzner. Arzner laughs throughout the filming.]

ARZNER: Thank you. You may return to your dressing rooms.

LINDSTROM: There are lost women.

END

Act Five

[*Lindstrom and Oberon exit.*]

[*Cohn enters. Oberon and Lindstrom exit. Arzner does not see Cohn.*]

ARZNER: [*making a frame with her hands*] Print it, please. One take. [*laughing*] One take.

[*Arzner walks toward a screen, tries to walk into the screen. She cannot. Arzner wails, pulls down the screen, but the light from the projector bears down on Arzner. She picks up the screen, looks into it as if looking into a mirror.*]

ARZNER: Am I in here?

[*Cohn opens Arzner's camera and rips out the film, destroying it. Arzner takes the destroyed film in her hands.*]

ARZNER: We call it a picture show, but it's so many pictures. You can't count them. Pictures as small as your eye, spinning. Evidence of the speed of light. [*she cries, pulling lengths of film between her fingers, staring into the blackened, exposed film*]
Three seconds. Her hair is black and someone has to touch it, because I cannot.
Four seconds. Her legs are as long as the screen can hold. Her skirt is grey and green. She's running. Like me.
Twelve seconds. A hard slap. Someone will kiss the skin where it's hot, because I'm not allowed.
Twenty seconds. A close-up of her face. Perfect. She's got one eye closed and one eye open. Her face is crying. She knows me, she spells out my name with her tears.

COHN: You're fired.

ARZNER: [crying, showing a length of film to Cohn] In this scene, she makes me happy.

COHN: Dotty, stop, please. I should dig my own eyes out.

ARZNER: [frames Cohn's face with her hands] I tried to walk into my own movie, Harry. I got caught.

COHN: You need to rest. Come back in a few months and start a new picture.

ARZNER: No, I'm leaving. Really leaving. It's over. [filming her surroundings with her hands] This is a good location for fade to credits. The shade is gorgeous ... black ... unforgiving, friendless black.

COHN: Aw, Dotty, why don't you slug me or something? [laughs uncomfortably]

ARZNER: [drops hand camera] I'm not in this scene.

[Cohn exits. Theme music from the radio show builds. Arzner pulls the cardigan she wore in the Prologue over her shoulder. She rests her face against the shiny reflection of the tabletop. The red 'On Air' light clicks on over her head.]

VOICE-OVER: Please join us next week when Westinghouse Radio Theatre and the 1955 Cadillac Convertible proudly present You Were Meant To Be a Star, with your host, Miss Dorothy Arzner.

[The 'On Air' light clicks off.]

ARZNER: [staring at reflection] I know you. [laughs] May you forever remain a secret. I'd rather I did.

END

Coda: A Conversation Between Dorothy Arzner and Pam Cook

[*To be presented to the audience following an intermission as a kind of 'artists' talk' after a production, but with the actors staying in character.*

The setting is Arzner's home in the desert, in 1975.Arzner enters, dressed in a skirt and jacket, carrying gardening gloves. She fixes her jacket and pats her hair, waiting for Cook. She finds her walking cane, and decides to hide it from sight. She changes her mind, setting the cane before her chair. Cook enters, carrying a tape recorder and a notepad. They shake hands.]

ARZNER: Miss Cook?

COOK: Pam, please, it's Pam.

ARZNER: If you like.

COOK: [*taking both of Arzner's hands*] I can't tell you what a pleasure this is for me. You, you're exactly the way I imagined you'd be.

ARZNER: [*uncomfortable with handholding*] What a comfort, for you. [*dropping Cook's hand*] You'll pardon me, Miss Cook, I'm too old to dance.

COOK: Oh, oh! Of course, please sit down!

ARZNER: I believe that is my line. [*pause*] Let's both sit down.

[*They sit.*]

COOK: I don't know where to begin. I have so many questions. I'm so honoured. I've wanted to meet you for years. Your home is lovely. I have seen all of your films, several times. Your work –

ARZNER: Pardon me, Miss Cook. I do not wish to appear inhospitable, but if you intend to spend the afternoon showering me with praise, perhaps you could simply tape record your adorations and I could go back to my flowers.

COOK: [nervously] I'm a little nervous.

ARZNER: No, you're excited. The difference grows more apparent as you age. [pause]
Forgive me, I'm an old woman with a bad temper. There is no other kind. Perhaps you had best ask me a question.

COOK: [with notes, sets tape recorder to 'Record'] Thank you. I'd like to start by asking you about the central problem, or rather problematization, buried in the narrative superstructure of your films – specifically, how your films are important in that they foreground the desires of women caught in systems of representation that allow them the opportunity to play, indeed to subvert, the specific demands of the dominant system.

ARZNER: Miss Cook, do you always speak this way?

COOK: Yes.

ARZNER: It seems like rather a lot of work simply to ask me how I managed for so many years to not get caught. In my day, all a woman had to do to be taken seriously was put on a pair of pants, not speak in tongues.

COOK: You mentioned getting caught?

ARZNER: [sighs] You are asking me how I made so many movies about intelligent, aggressive women and sold them to the studios, to the world, as sob-sister 'women's pictures', are you not?

COOK: Traditional Hollywood films are dominated by the male gaze.

ARZNER: There is your answer – I am not male.

COOK: But the art form is – the single eye of the camera, the way films are composed, frame by individual frame, like a mathematics table, all in a linear, formal pattern – cinema mimics the thinking patterns of male psychology. It's built into the technology. The camera is a man's eye.

ARZNER: I was told such nonsense thirty years ago, and I still resist the idea. If I proved anything in my work, it is that technology does not possess a sex. Technology is neutral. Whatever viewpoints appear on the screen are either the individual visions of the director, or, more often, the unfulfilled needs of the audience.

COOK: Are you saying I'm suffering from projection?

ARZNER: Tell me something, Miss Cook, is it not easier for you and your female colleagues to believe that movies are a force unto themselves, that they live and breathe independently of their makers? Is that fantasy not much easier to believe than the idea that perhaps I made some ridiculous, melodramatic and even foolish films, as you say, 'within the system', because I wanted to? Because I enjoyed myself?

COOK: Then why did you leave, why didn't you finish your last film?

ARZNER: I was suffering from pneumonia. Surely you read that in your research.

COOK: That's the official reason.

ARZNER: [testy] And the only one I have to offer. Your generation automatically assumes official reasons are lies. My generation knew how to mind its own business.

COOK: [nervous] I apologize, I didn't mean to imply –

ARZNER: Pneumonia was much more difficult to cure then than it is today ... it sometimes took years to regain one's ... one's health.

COOK: [pats Arzner's knee] Well, you're in great shape now.

ARZNER: I am 77 years old and by all rights I should pass away at any moment. [takes Cooks hand, squeezes it] Ask me another question.

COOK: Were you aware of the effects of your films at the time they were shown?

ARZNER: I was in New York in 1934, and I noticed dozens of women on 5th Avenue wearing hats exactly like the hats I had had designed for my picture with Katharine Hepburn. It was a very valuable lesson about the edifying powers of cinema.

COOK: Now you're teasing me.

ARZNER: Louis B. Mayer once said to me, 'Movies are for entertainment. If you want to send a message, send a telegram'. I thought this quite clever, until I heard him repeat it for fifteen years.

COOK: But your films are loaded with political and social subtexts.

ARZNER: All of them completely irrelevant. Audiences consumed motion pictures in those years the same way people poison themselves with cheaply produced food today. Any nourishment was accidental.

COOK: Then you admit to an agenda.

ARZNER: I admit to doing my job.

COOK: But my study of your films turns up a recurring pattern – whenever the story dictated that the hero and the heroine fall in love, you found subtle ways to show the audience that the woman was not truly happy. Your camera work cleverly dodges and obscures images of male–female love, you consistently undermined the heterosexual orthodoxy.

ARZNER: You are on a very wrong tack, Miss Cook. I was not sneaking about, inserting secret messages and childish, ungrateful, low blows. I was working out a coherent vision. I was very fortunate to be given the artist's privilege of exploring a recurring theme, which was simply that a woman is never secure or completely whole when she is in love.

But that is not enough for young women today, to take another woman's word when she tells you she was glad to do the work given to her. You must find contradictions, you must unearth something rotten and dark! You talk about your respect for my work, yet you make me out to be little more than a third-rate kitchen maid stealing silver from my masters, and then you expect me to be grateful for the comparison! *[pause]*

Furthermore, there is no sexual orthodoxy of any kind – it is all delusional talk – one does what one does as time and place and opportunity dictate.

COOK: But as a lesbian making heterosexual love stories –

ARZNER: I am not a lesbian.

COOK: *[exasperated]* Then, as a pioneering feminist –

ARZNER: 'Feminist' is a careless and inaccurate term. *[begins to rise from her chair]* I'm getting tired, Miss Cook.

COOK: Miss Arzner, please ... I've come such a long way to see you.

ARZNER: Thirty-two years ago I was forced to behave myself. Now, another group of well-wishers such as yourself would like me to reform a second time. Once again, other people are deciding who I am. Well, this is my home. I am in no one's employ. I reserve my right to remain exclusively myself. Isn't that the same right you and your friends are demanding?

COOK: It's not wrong to look for allies. Women deserve to know their own history.

ARZNER: [*rising, shakes Cook's hand*] At my expense? No, Miss Cook, I'd rather be left alone. Watch my films, write whatever you see. Pretend I'm dead.

COOK: [*standing*] I don't believe you. I think it bothers you that you've been forgotten ... I'm sorry, I didn't mean –

ARZNER: You'll excuse me now, my flowers need watering. They suffer terribly when they're misremembered. Most things do.

[*Arzner exits. Cook hesitates, takes tape out of recorder and leaves it on a table. Cook exits.*]

END

Production Notes

Camera, Woman debuted at Buddies in Bad Times Theatre in Toronto on October 14, 1998, in a co-production between Buddies in Bad Times and The Simmer Company.

Camera, Woman was directed by Franco Boni, with assistance from Laura Cowell. The cast included Sarah Stanley as Dorothy Arzner, Veronika Hurnik as Merle Oberon, Sam Malkin as Harry Cohn, Ellen-Ray Hennessy as Louella Parsons, Caroline Gillis as Rose Lindstrom, and Ellen-Ray Hennessy as Pam Cook.

The original set was designed by Adrian Blackwell, with film projections by Laura Cowell. Costumes and makeup were designed by Sarah Armstrong. The original sound design was created by Darren Copeland, and the lighting was designed by Andrea Lundy.

Acknowledgements

Thanks and love to Sky Gilbert, Sarah Stanley and Gwen Bartleman for their unwavering faith. Special thanks to Kirsten Johnson, Peter Lynch, Moynan King and Paul Forsyth, good friends and even better listeners.

Typeset in Cartier Book
at Coach House Printing on bpNichol Lane, 2000

Edited by Darren Wershler-Henry
Copy edited and proofread by Alana Wilcox
Designed by Darren Wershler-Henry and damian lopes
Cover design by Rick/Simon
Cover photo by Guntar Kravis
Author photo by Paul Forsyth

To read the online version of this text and other titles from
Coach House Books, visit our website:
www.chbooks.com

To add your name to our e-mailing list, write:
mail@chbooks.com

Toll-free:
1 800 376 6360

Coach House Books
401 Huron Street (rear) on bpNichol Lane
Toronto, Ontario
M5S 2G5